Mrs. Harriet Anne De Salis

Oysters à la mode, or, The Oyster and over 100 ways of Cooking it

to which are added a few Recipes for Cooking all kinds of shellfish

Mrs. Harriet Anne De Salis

Oysters à la mode, or, The Oyster and over 100 ways of Cooking it
to which are added a few Recipes for Cooking all kinds of shellfish

ISBN/EAN: 9783744789691

Printed in Europe, USA, Canada, Australia, Japan

Cover: Foto ©Andreas Hilbeck / pixelio.de

More available books at **www.hansebooks.com**

OYSTERS À LA MODE

OR

THE OYSTER AND OVER 100 WAYS OF COOKING IT

TO WHICH ARE ADDED A FEW

RECIPES FOR COOKING ALL KINDS OF SHELLFISH

BY

MRS DE SALIS

AUTHORESS OF 'SAVOURIES À LA MODE' 'ENTRÉES À LA MODE'
'SOUP AND FISH À LA MODE' 'SWEETS AND
SUPPER DISHES À LA MODE'

'O rare invertebrate! thy praise be mine.
What joy lies within that crusty coat!
What power to please the palate e'er is thine!
What welcome waits thee from th' impatient throat!
Stewed, fried, or roasted, panned or on the shell,
Or broiled—no matter how they choose to serve thee,
Thy odours all my senses quick compel,
And for a gastronomic battle nerve me.
No dainty yet prepared on earth's broad range
Can match thee fresh from out thy pearly cloister.
Thy name? we'll breathe it—Shakespeare's line to change—
Unrivalled dainty! sure thy name is Oyster'

The Family Doctor

LONDON
LONGMANS, GREEN, AND CO.
AND NEW YORK : 15 EAST 16th STREET
1888

PREFACE.

THERE is a saying 'Dumb as an Oyster.' It may be dumb, but that is no reason why its lovers should be so; and therefore, in bringing a little volume before the public on the subject of oysters, and the numerous ways in which they can be cooked, I do *not* wish to be dumb, and I trust my readers will receive this little work as kindly as they have done my previous ones.

Personally I agree with the many who consider oysters are best when served in their homely shell ; but there are many who prefer them in gorgeous and fancy dresses, and for these there will be found plenty of oyster costumes in this little book.

Several of the recipes are original, and I hope that the result of a trial of them will prove as satisfactory to connoisseurs as those which I have culled from celebrated authorities.

HARRIET A. DE SALIS.

INTRODUCTION.

THE oyster (Latin, *ostracea*, *ostreidæ* or *pectinidæ*) is of the family of Conchiferous Mollusca to which the common oyster or *ostrea edulis* belongs, and is described as a bivalve shellfish having the valves generally unequal. The hinge is without teeth, but furnished with a somewhat oval cavity, and mostly with lateral grooves ; they generally adhere to rocks, or, as in two or three species, to roots of trees on the shore.

The 'ostrea edulis' may be said to have its home in Britain, for though found elsewhere on the coasts of Europe, and other countries, in no part does it attain such perfection as in *our* seas.

The ancient Romans valued our native oysters even as we do now, and must have held them in higher estimation than those of Italian shores, or they would not have brought them so far for their luxurious feasts. Juvenal records the exquisite taste of the epicure

Who
At the first bite each oyster's birthplace knew,
Whether a Lucrine or Circæan he'd bitten,
Or one from Rutupinian deeps in Britain.

Essex and Suffolk are the most celebrated localities in England for them, where they are dredged up by means of a net with an iron scraper at the mouth, which is dragged by a rope from a boat over the beds. As soon as they are taken from their native beds, they are stored in pits, made for the purpose, furnished with sluices, through which at the spring tides the water is suffered to flow. This water being stagnant soon becomes green in warm weather, and in a few days afterwards the oysters acquire the same tinge, which increases their value in the market. They do not, however, attain their perfection, and become fit for *sale*, till the end of six or eight weeks. They are not considered proper for the table till they are about a year and a half old, so that the brood of one spring are not to be taken for sale till at least the September twelve months afterwards.

The more delicate and smallest kinds are called natives, and are used for eating; the coarser kinds are called the deep-sea oysters, and are dredged for, and are used for cooking. There are several kinds of oysters. Of the former, which we receive from Milton, Colchester, and the vicinity of those places, the Ostend, Anglo-Dutch, Arcachon, and the celebrated Rocher de Cancale and Burton Bindons Red Bank are the best.

A very singular circumstance, not generally known, is that the finest oysters we have in England and Ireland both come from a place with the same name, viz. from Burnham, Essex, in England, and from Burnham, co. Clare, in Ireland. Of the deep-sea oysters those that are unfed are the best, as their flavour is stronger and their flesh is firmer. Real lovers of oysters maintain that no oyster is worth eating till it is quite two years old. Their age is known by their shell, just the same as the age of a tree is known by its bark, or a fish by its scale, and the smaller the oyster the finer its flavour

Many esteem the Colchester Pyfleet as the best, though the native Milton is reckoned the fattest and whitest. They are known to be alive and vigorous when they close fast upon the knife, and let go as soon as they are wounded in the body.

The oyster fishery in Britain is esteemed of so much importance that it is regulated by a Court of Admiralty, and, according to law, oysters come into season on August 4, and go out the beginning of May, which justifies the old saying that they are to be eaten whenever there is the letter R in the month.

In the month of May the fishermen are allowed to take the oysters, in order to separate the spawn from the cultch, the latter of which is thrown in again to preserve the bed for the future. After this month it is felony to carry away the cultch, and otherwise punishable to take any oyster between the shells of which, when closed, a shilling will rattle.

The French assert that the English oysters, which are esteemed the best in Europe, were originally procured from Cancale Bay, near St. Malo, but they assign no proof of this. It is a fact, however, that the oysters eaten in ancient Rome were nourished in the channel which then parted the Isle of Thanet from England, and which has since been filled up and converted into meadows.

There is much diversity of opinion about the wholesomeness and the nutritive powers of oysters. Some medical men say that they, like all shellfish, afford but a small amount of nutritive substance, which is the reason why a great many can be eaten without spoiling the appetite for other dishes.

In former days a dinner of any pretension always began with oysters, and *many* of the guests never stopped till they had swallowed a gross, *i.e.*

144 oysters. The 'Almanach des Gourmands' (1803) states that 'beyond five or six dozen, as a mere indispensable prelude to a winter *déjeuner*, it is proved that oyster eating most certainly ceases to be an enjoyment.'

Brillat-Savarin once weighed a dozen oysters, and found they weighed four ounces, which gives for the weight of a gross three pounds, and remarked that the same persons who dined were not a bit the worse after their oysters, who would have been completely satiated had they eaten an equal quantity of any meat, however delicate.

He also relates that, in 1798, when he was at Versailles in the capacity of a commissioner of the Directory, that he was frequently thrown in the way of the Sieur Laporte, clerk to the Tribunal of the Department, who was excessively fond of oysters, and often complained that he had never had 'his fill of them.'

Brillat-Savarin resolved to procure him this gratification, and invited him to dine.

They both ate three dozen, and then Brillat-Savarin had to stop, but the Sieur went on alone ; but when he had arrived at the thirty-second dozen, his host was getting so tired of the game of looking on, he at last exclaimed, ' My very dear fellow, I see it is not written that you are to have your fill of oysters to-day ; let us begin our dinner,' and when they began the Sieur dined ' with the vigour of a man who had fasted for twelve hours previously !'

Dr. Spencer Thomson, in speaking of the nutritive powers and wholesomeness of the oyster, says that when uncooked they are especially wholesome, but their digestibility in all probability depends greatly upon the person by whom they are eaten.

Some, whose stomachs generally require much con-
sideration, can eat oysters with impunity. Dr.
Paris, however, condemns them for invalids. It is
said that if a cupful of hot milk is taken by delicate
persons immediately after eating them, it will greatly
assist their digestion. The Rev. J. G. Wood, who
has written a good deal on the subject of the oyster,
says, in regard to eating them, ' As to such heresies
as pepper and vinegar, let them be banished from
the table, whilst oysters are upon it. These charm-
ing mollusks should always be taken unmitigated,
without losing the delicacy of their flavour by a
mixture with any condiment whatever except their
native juice. Scarcely one man in a thousand knows
how to open an oyster, and still less how to eat it.

' The ordinary system which is employed at the
oyster shops is radically false, for all the juice is
lost, and the oyster is left to become dry and insipid
upon the flat shell, which effectually answers as a
drain to convey off the liquid, which is to the
oyster what the milk is to the cocoa-nut. Those
who wish to eat oysters as they should be eaten
should act as follows. Hold the mollusk firmly in
a cloth, insert the point of a knife neatly just before
the edge of the upper shell, give a quick decided
pressure till the point is felt to glide along the
polished inner surface of the under shell ; force it
sharply to the hinge, give a smart wrench rather
towards the right hand, and off comes the shell.
Then pass the knife quickly under the oyster,
separate it from its attachment, let it fall into the
lower shell, floating in its juice, lift it quickly to
the lips, and eat it before the delicate aroma has
been dissipated into the atmosphere. There is as
much difference between an oyster thus opened

and eaten, as between champagne frothing and leaping out of the silver-necked bottle, and the same wine after it has been allowed to stand for six hours with the cork removed. There is another method of eating oysters, wherein no knife is required, and not the least skill in opening is needed, the only requisite being a bright fire. You pick out a glowing spot in the fire, where there are no flames and no black pieces of coal to dart jets of smoke exactly in the place where they are not wanted. You then insert a row of oysters into the glowing coals, taking care to keep their mouths outward and within an easy grasp of the tongs, and their convexity downwards. Presently a spitting and hissing noise is heard, which gradually increases till the shells begin to open and the juice is seen boiling merrily within, the mollusk itself becoming whiter and more opaque as the operation continues. There is no rule for ascertaining the precise point at which the cooking is completed, for every one has his own taste, and must learn by personal experience. A little practice soon makes perfect, and the expert operator will be able to keep up a continual supply as fast as he can manage to eat them. When they are thoroughly cooked they should be taken from the fire, a second batch inserted, and the still hissing and spluttering mollusks be eaten " scorching hot." . . . No one who has not eaten oysters dressed in this primitive mode has the least idea of the piquant flavour of which they are capable. Stewed in their own juice, the action of fire only brings out the full flavour, and as the juice is consumed as well as the oyster, there is no waste and no dissipation of the indescribable but potent aroma.'

OYSTERS À LA MODE.

Oyster Aigrettes.
Aigrettes aux Huîtres.

PUT one ounce of butter into half a pint of cold water till it boils ; when boiling add two and a half ounces of Vienna flour, stirring vigorously all the time over the fire until it is cooked, that is to say, until the panada leaves the sides of the saucepan quite clean and coats the spoon. Take it off the fire, and when slightly cooled add two whole eggs and the yolk of another, one by one, a little salt and cayenne, a teaspoonful of lemon-juice, and then three ounces of oyster powder,[1] and beat well together. Have ready some fat not quite boiling, and drop small pieces of the mixture from a teaspoon and fry till a nice brown : it generally takes five to ten minutes. Serve on a napkin in form of a pyramid, and sprinkle with oyster powder dried in the oven.

Angels on Horseback.
Huîtres à Cheval.

Take *very thin* slices of fat bacon ; cut all the rind off. Then take an oyster (or two if very smally ;

[1] *See* Oyster Powder.

B

pour on it two drops of essence of anchovy, four of lemon and a dust of cayenne, and roll it in the slice of bacon ; when there are sufficient of these rolls, put them on a small skewer and fry them ; when cooked, take each one separately and place on a fried croûton.   This is a dish which must be served very hot.

Aspic of Oysters.
Huîtres en Aspic.

Make some aspic jelly ; have ready two dozen oysters, bearded and blanched in their own liquor ; cut them in halves ; boil three eggs hard, a few leaves of chervil, and four boned anchovies.   Put a layer of the jelly in the mould, then arrange six whole oysters on it ; then, when cool, another layer of jelly ; then arrange the half oysters, eggs cut in rings, and the anchovies cut into dice alternately in designs, placing here and there a chervil leaf. Put in more jelly, and so on till the mould is full, when it must be put on ice, and when stiff turned out and garnished with lemon sippets, parsley, and crayfish.

Attelets of Oysters.
Attelets aux Huîtres.

Stew the oysters as for oyster sauce.   Have a sauce made as follows.   Fry some herbs in a little butter, put a spoonful of flour in, moisten with the strained liquor of the oysters, season well with a little cayenne and salt, reduce the sauce, and thicken it with the yolks of three eggs, and pour it over the oysters.   Let the whole stand till cold, and then skewer the oysters, using silver skewers, and with a knife spread the sauce all round. Throw grated bread-crumbs over the oysters ; next dip into a batter, and then into crumbs again. Fry them of a fine brown, and serve.

Oysters and Bacon (a Breakfast Dish).
Huîtres au Lard.

Fry up some mashed potatoes in bacon fat, and break them in pieces with a fork, and let them brown a little more ; cut some thin rashers of bacon and arrange round the potatoes, which should be piled up in the middle of the dish. Broil some oysters in their shells with butter and cayenne, turn them out of their shells and place on the top of the potatoes ; garnish with lemon sippets. Ham may be used instead of bacon.

Baked Oysters.
Huîtres au Four.

Mix three tablespoonfuls of finely-grated bread-crumbs with half a saltspoonful of white pepper and a grate of nutmeg.

Beard a dozen oysters, dip them in beaten egg, roll them in the seasoned crumbs, put each one in its lower shell, and lay a small piece of butter upon it. Place the oysters in the oven for a few minutes until they are quite hot. Before serving, squeeze a little lemon-juice over them.

Oysters in Batter.
Huîtres à la Française.

Take some oysters, beard them, strain the liquor, and put them to stand in it for ten minutes.

B 2

Mix smoothly some butter, two tablespoonfuls of flour ; add to it, stirring till quite smooth, a little milk and cream mixed together ; beat up the yolk of an egg, and stir in with it a little salt, beat the white to a froth, and add just before using ; it must be as thick as very good cream. Take about a dessertspoonful of the batter, put an oyster into the centre, and drop it into a frying-pan in which you have some boiling lard ; as they are done, put them on paper before the fire to drain.

If preferred, a French batter may be made with three tablespoonfuls of flour, a little salt, a few drops of oil or beer, and mix with tepid water *very* lightly, or it will not drop from the spoon as it should ; whisk the whites of two eggs to a froth and stir in ; dip each oyster in. This batter is lighter than the other.

Oysters boiled au Beurre.
Huîtres bouillies au Beurre.

Wash the shells carefully, throw them into a saucepan of boiling water, and let them boil quickly for three or four minutes ; then take them up and serve in the shells with melted butter in a tureen.

Little Bombs of Oysters à la Gourmet.
Petites Bombes d'Huîtres à la Gourmet.

Take some small moulds and line them thinly with aspic jelly, and ornament at the top with a curled fillet of anchovy skinned, and round the middle of the mould arrange a row of lobster coral, and form a border at the base with pieces of caviare and anchovy. Mask the garnish all over with more aspic jelly, and fill up the moulds with a purée of oysters made of two dozen bearded oysters, three boned anchovies, a dust of cayenne, a teaspoonful of strained lemon-juice, and a good tablespoonful of cream ; pound these well together and pass through a hair sieve ; mix with this purée two gills of whipped aspic and a gill of stiffly whipped cream, and set aside till firm. When cold turn the moulds and dish up on a border of chopped aspic jelly ornamented with chervil.

Oyster Bouchées à l'Allemande.
Bouchées d'Huîtres à l'Allemande.

Have some little bouchée cups lined with puff paste, and bake them in a brisk oven. Take two dozen blanched oysters and ten turned mushrooms. Cut the whole into dice, and warm them in some Allemande sauce ; fill the bouchées, and cover with fried parsley over which a little lemon-juice has been squeezed.

Huîtres à la Brochette.
Oysters à la Brochette.

Remove some large oysters from their shells, toss them in bread-crumbs previously seasoned with pepper and salt, and a little finely-minced parsley.

Place them in a double gridiron, sprinkle them with dissolved butter ; grill them for one minute. Dish them in a circle on a napkin, with fried parsley in the centre. Serve thin slices of brown bread and butter and lemon cut in quarters with them.

Oysters Broiled.
Huîtres Grillées.

Take a dozen oysters, open them, and leave them in the deep shell. Place a little butter upon each, with a pinch of salt and cayenne, and half a teaspoonful of lemon-juice. Put the shells on the gridiron over a clear but not fierce fire, and boil them for three minutes. Serve them neatly arranged on a folded napkin. Serve with brown bread and butter.

Oysters Browned (in their own Gravy).
Huîtres au Jus.

Take a dozen plump and good-sized oysters ; as they are opened, pour their liquor carefully into a cup. Beard the oysters, sprinkle a little pepper and salt over them, and dip each one separately into the yolk of an egg which has been mixed smoothly with a teaspoonful of flour. Brown them in a saucepan with a little clarified butter ; lift them out, mix their liquor with the butter, and thicken it with half a teaspoonful of flour. Simmer gently for three minutes, stir in the browned oysters, let them get hot ; then serve them on toasted bread on a hot dish.

Oyster Butter.
Beurre aux Huîtres.

Pound eighteen oysters in a mortar with a little lemon-juice, a little cayenne pepper, and twice their weight of butter. Rub through a sieve, and put in a cool place till wanted ; then use the butter hands, and make them into little balls ; dish in a pryamid, and hand brown bread and butter and shred celery with it.

Oysters in Cases à la Toulouse.
Huîtres en Caisses à la Toulouse.

Steep one pound of new bread in tepid water, wring it in a cloth to extract the moisture, put it into a stewpan with an ounce of butter and a little salt, stir it over the fire with a wooden spoon till it leaves the sides of the pan ; then scald and beard two dozen oysters, an ounce and a half of the bread panada, one ounce of butter, and the yolk of three eggs ; pound all in a mortar, then rub through a wire sieve ; add one gill of the oyster liquor and one of whipped cream, season with a dust of cayenne pepper and salt, the squeeze of a lemon, the whipped whites of two eggs beaten to snow. Mix the whole lightly, and pour into little moulds or paper cases which have been brushed with dissolved butter ; place buttered paper over, and steam for about half an hour.

Oyster Canapes.
Canapés aux Huîtres.

Cut little rounds of bread, fry them a pale colour, and lay on each two oysters bearded ; dust slightly with cayenne, and squeeze two drops of lemon on each ; whip some cream and pour over.

These can be varied by putting whipped aspic over instead of the cream.

Oyster Cannelons à la Whitstable.
Cannelons d'Huîtres à la Whitstable.

Chop up some oysters that have been soaking in lemon-juice, add a few mushrooms, and mix the whole in some stiffly reduced Allemande sauce. Roll out some seven turns puff paste to about one-eighth of an inch thickness. Moisten the surface with a brush dipped in water; place some equally sized portions of the above mixture on the paste, about two inches long by one inch; enclose each portion with paste. Press the edges together, and roll these cannelons on the board to a cork shape; fry them in warm fat. Drain, and dish them on a napkin, garnish with fried parsley, and serve.

Oyster and Caviare Sandwiches.
Tartines d'Huîtres et Caviar.

Cut thin slices of brown bread and butter; cover one piece thinly with caviare, then put on some whole fresh oysters, cover with the other piece of bread and butter, and form into a sandwich. The oysters must not be cut, and there should be two in each sandwich. A squeeze of lemon is a great improvement.

Chartreuse of Oysters.
Chartreuse d'Huîtres.

Take three or four dozen oysters, beard them and take away the hard parts or horns; add half a pint of strained oyster liquor, a glass of chablis, and five or six anchovies boned and minced; let·them simmer. When warm strain the liquor, and add to it eight or ten sheets of best French leaf gelatine, melted in a gill of oyster liquor, with a good pinch of white pepper ; boil it up and clarify it with whites of eggs, tammy it, and then add a little of Marshall's apple-green colouring. Now have two plain moulds, one about one inch larger than the other, and pour a very little of the jelly into the bottom of the larger one ; then place on it a layer of the oysters, with pieces of the anchovies here and there ; cover this with more jelly, but only just enough to make a smooth surface ; lay this on ice. When it is quite firm put the smaller mould inside the larger one, taking care to place it exactly in the middle, so that the vacant space may be the same all round. In this vacant place dispose of the rest of the oysters and anchovies, filling up the interstices with jelly till the whole mould is filled up. Place the mould upon ice to freeze, and when ready to turn out fill the inner mould with warm water, and then pull it out and fill up the inner space with iced lobster sauce, and turn out the entire mould. Garnish with red aspic jelly.

Oysters Cold au Naturel.

The true lover of oysters will prefer them without any adjuncts except their own gravy, but still there are many who like to have vinegar and pepper, or lemon and cayenne, as accompaniments. Brown bread and butter is usually served with them ; stout or chablis is generally drunk with them.

Oyster Cream.
Huîtres à la Crème.

Pound four dozen oysters in a mortar, taking away the hard parts; add a little of their liquor, a dust of cayenne, and half a pint of double cream whilst pounding; add pepper and salt to taste. Pass the mixture through a hair sieve and work in another half-pint of cream. Garnish a plain mould with truffles and pistachio nuts; pour in the mixture, and steam for an hour very slowly. Serve with chablis or champagne sauce, and lemon sippets. Small moulds may be used instead of the larger one.

Oyster Creams à la Devonshire.
Crème d'Huîtres à la Devonshire.

Take some fresh oysters, beard them, and cover each with three drops of essence of anchovy and a squeeze of lemon and a tiny dust of cayenne. Have some Devonshire clotted cream, and stir in these oysters. Put three with some cream into the little French china ramequin moulds, and strew lobster coral over the top and serve.

Croquettes of Oysters.
Croquettes aux Huîtres.

Take a dozen plump large oysters. Put them in their own liquor in a saucepan over a gentle fire for a minute or two to harden; then beard them; then cut each one into eight or ten pieces. .Mix an ounce of butter smoothly in a stewpan with half an ounce of flour, add the oyster liquor, a dust of cayenne, a teaspoonful of anchovy sauce, a grate of nutmeg, and a gill of milk. Stir these ingredients over the fire until the sauce is smooth and thick; lift the pan off the fire for a minute, and add a teaspoonful of good gravy, the yolks of two eggs well-beaten, and a teaspoonful of lemon-juice. Stir the sauce again over the fire till the eggs are set. Then add the oysters, let them get *quite hot*, spread the mixture upon a plate about one and a half inches thick, and put it aside to get cold. Strew some finely-grated bread-crumbs on a board, divide the oyster mixture into equal sized parts, roll these to the shape of balls, egg and bread-crumb them, and fry them in hot fat till crisp and of a pale colour. Pile them up on a napkin and garnish with fried parsley.

Curried Oysters.

Kari aux Huîtres.

Put one to two ounces of butter into a saucepan; when it boils add an onion cut in very thin slices, let it fry; then stir in one to two tablespoonfuls of curry powder according to the quantity you wish to have; make it smooth, stirring with a wooden spoon; add your stock with oyster liquor in it quite hot. Mix well, cover the pan, and let the whole boil. Now put in the oysters, and the strained juice of half a lemon. Let this simmer gently, stirring now and then with a wooden spoon, and serve very hot. Boiled rice should be served in another dish.

Indian Oysters Curried.
Huîtres à l'Inde.

Open and beard two dozen large oysters and preserve their liquor. Mince an onion finely, and fry it in an ounce of butter till tender. Stir into it a heaped dessertspoonful of curry powder, add a little more butter, and pour in gradually a gill of nicely seasoned stock. When the mixture boils stir in some desiccated cocoa-nut, about a tablespoonful, and a small sour apple finely minced. Simmer gently till the apple is dissolved ; then thicken the gravy with a little flour, and season with pepper and salt. Put in the oysters with their liquor, and half of the milk of a cocoa-nut. Let all this stew for a few minutes, stirring it gently all the time ; then add a teaspoonful of strained lemon-juice. Serve with a border of boiled rice.

Oyster Cutlets.
Côtelettes d'Huîtres.

Take half a pound of lean and nicely cooked veal, two ounces of butter, half a pound of large stewing oysters. After the beards have been cut away, mince all very small, and pound in a mortar. Soak three tablespoonfuls of bread-crumbs in the liquor of the oysters, and mix with veal mixture ; season with salt, pepper, a dust of cayenne, the juice of half a lemon ; add the beaten yolks of two eggs to the above, and mix all thoroughly. Make up in the shape of small cutlets, egg and bread-crumb them, and fry them. Drain well, and serve in a circle with fried parsley in the centre.   .

Oyster Cutlets à la Chef.
Côtelettes d'Huîtres à la Chef.

Mix about half a pound of veal with the same weight of large stewing oysters ; chop all very finely and then pound them together in a mortar, adding two ounces of finely-chopped veal suet and three tablespoonfuls of bread-crumbs which have been soaked in the oyster liquor. Season with a little salt, white pepper, and a teaspoonful of lemon-juice. Now add the beaten yolks of two eggs, and mix thoroughly, pounding a little more, and make up into the shape of small cutlets. Fry them in butter, after dipping them in egg and bread-crumbs.

Drain them well, and send to table very hot. Garnish with sprigs of parsley, and slices of lemon cut into fancy shapes.

Devilled Oysters.
Huîtres au Diable.

When the oysters are opened (choose large ones) retain them and their liquor in the deep shell. Insert cayenne pepper and salt to taste, and put the shells on a gridiron with a piece of butter on the top of each oyster. With a clear bright fire it will take three to four minutes to cook them.

Brown bread and butter should accompany them.

Dutch Oysters.
Huîtres à la Flamande.

Roll rock oysters in yolk of egg, then dip them in grated bread-crumbs, and white pepper one by one and fry them in butter. Serve with white sauce in which the liquor from the oysters has been strained, and the juice of a lemon.

Oyster Etiquettes.
Etiquettes d'Huîtres.

Open two dozen oysters and put them in a basin ; chop a small bunch of parsley very fine. Mix with it a little minced lemon-peel, a quarter of a nutmeg grated, a dust of cayenne, the crumb of a French roll grated fine ; beat the yolks of three eggs, dip each oyster separately into this, and then roll them in bread-crumbs until they are thoroughly encased ; put three ounces of butter into a Dutch oven before a brisk fire, and when the butter is melted, arrange the oysters on the tray of the oven, and keep them turned till they are perfectly browned. Serve them with bread and butter cut very thin, and a stick of celery.

Fleur of Oysters au Cordon Bleu.
Fleur d'Huîtres au Cordon Bleu.

Butter a round flower shape, and place it on a buttered paper in a baking tin ; then line it with a mixture of four ounces of Vienna flour mixed into a stiff paste with two ounces of butter, one egg, a teaspoonful of lemon-juice, and a dust of cayenne, or a little green colouring mixed with a little cold water, and line the flower shape with it, and put in a buttered paper cut to its shape ; fill this with barley, and cook it in the oven for a quarter of an hour ; then take out the barley, fold a band of paper round the shape as if it

were a soufflé, and fill up the flower with the fol-
lowing preparation.

One ounce of flour, one ounce of butter, a little
cayenne, a dessertspoonful of strained lemon-juice,
two yolks of eggs, a tablespoonful of cream, half a
gill of chablis, six drops of anchovy sauce ; stir all
these over the fire till they boil. Then mix in four
boned anchovies chopped very small, two dozen
oysters that have been scalded in their own liquor,
and the whipped whites of two eggs. Pour this
into the mould, and sprinkle over a few bread-
crumbs and some butter broken in pieces on the
top, and bake for twenty minutes. Garnish with
parsley sprinkled on the top, and slices of lemon
on the dish.

Fillets of Soles with Oysters.
Filets de Soles aux Huîtres.

Take eight fillets of soles, and cook them in a
buttered sauté-pan, and dish them round a croustade
filled with oysters, mixed in Allemande sauce.
Pour some of the same sauce over the fillets.

Fricasseed Oysters.
Huîtres en Fricassée.

Cut two ounces of lean ham into dice, and put
them into a stewpan with two ounces of fresh
butter, a bunch of parsley, a sprig of thyme, a sliced
onion, an inch of thin lemon-rind, and two cloves.
Place the cover on the pan and let the contents
steam gently for ten minutes. Pour over them
half a pint of stock or gravy thickened with a
spoonful of flour, a teaspoonful of essence of
anchovy, and let them simmer for twenty minutes.

Add two dozen oysters, and when they are quite hot draw the saucepan to the side of the fire for a minute or two to cool ; then gradually mix in the yolk of an egg, beaten up with a tablespoonful of cream. Simmer again for a minute, and serve the oysters on a hot dish with the sauce strained and poured over them. A teaspoonful of lemon-juice is an improvement.

Oysters Fried.
Huîtres Frites.

Take twelve to fourteen oysters, open them carefully, and put by the liquor from them ; put them into a stewpan over the fire in a little water to blanch for a few minutes (if there is enough liquor to warm them in, it is better than water) ; take out the oysters, keep the liquor, beard the oysters, and lay them on a sieve, then on to a cloth to dry. Break a fresh egg on a plate, beat well with a fork ; have about a quarter of a pound of bread-crumbs, to which has been added a spoonful of chopped parsley, a grate of nutmeg, a little pepper, and dust of cayenne. Dip each oyster first in the egg, then in the bread-crumbs. Put them into a small wire basket, fry for one minute in very hot lard.

Oysters Fried à l'Américaine.
Huîtres Frites à l'Américaine.

Choose the largest and best oysters you can find. Take them carefully from the liquor, lay them in rows upon a clean cloth, and press another lightly upon them to absorb the moisture.

Have ready several beaten eggs, and in another

dish some rusks crushed fine ; heat enough butter in the frying-pan to cover the oysters entirely. Dip each oyster first in the egg, then into the crushed rusks, rolling it over so that it may become completely encrusted. Drop them carefully in the frying-pan and fry quickly to a light brown. If the butter is hot enough, they will be soon ready to take out. Test it by putting in one oyster before the rest are risked. They must not lie in the pan an instant after they are done. Serve dry on a hot dish.

Oyster Fritters à l'Epicure.
Beignets d'Huîtres à l'Epicure.

Open a dozen oysters, and simmer them for two minutes in their own liquor. Beard them and put them aside. Beat two eggs, and mix with them half a tablespoonful of milk. Add a little salt, a quarter of a saltspoonful of pepper, a grate of nutmeg, and a quarter of a teaspoonful of lemon-rind. Dip the oysters in this batter, and then into finely-grated bread-crumbs. Fry in hot fat until they are brown and crisp. These can be eaten as a savoury, or can be used for garnishing.

Oyster Forcemeat.
Farce aux Huîtres.

Take one dozen oysters, beard them, strain the liquor, and scald the oysters in it ; chop them, and mix with them four ounces of bread-crumbs, one ounce and a half of butter, a small dessertspoonful of parsley finely minced, the grated rind of half a lemon, a dust of cayenne, and salt to taste. Mix

C

well, and bind with the yolk of an egg and a dessertspoonful of the oyster liquor.

Oysters au Gratin.

Huîtres au Gratin.

Put six ounces of macaroni into a stewpan with three pints of boiling water. Season with a pinch of salt and two pinches of pepper, and simmer for twenty minutes.

Drain the macaroni and put it back into the saucepan with half a pint of good gravy, and let it stew till the macaroni is tender and the gravy absorbed. Turn it out, chop it small, and put it again into the stewpan with a dozen or more of oysters, cut into small pieces, two ounces of grated Parmesan, one ounce of butter, a dust of cayenne, and as much gravy as will moisten it.

Shake the saucepan over the fire till the cheese is melted, then pile the macaroni high in a dish, sprinkle over it two ounces of Parmesan cheese and a dessertspoonful of browned bread-crumbs, pour over half an ounce of clarified butter, and brown the mixture in a gentle oven or before the fire.

Oysters au Gratin Superlatif.

Huîtres au Gratin Superlatif.

Scald the oysters in a saucepan in their own liquor, put them into silver or china scallop shells with a little sweet oil, season them with chopped shalot, parsley, and an anchovy minced fine, pepper and salt to taste, cover with fine bread-crumbs, and moisten with sweet oil. Put them into the oven for a few minutes, and brown them with a salamander and squeeze a few drops of lemon over them before serving.

Hashed Oysters.

Open twelve oysters, put the liquor in a stew-pan, and the oysters in a saucepan, and when nearly boiling take them out and put them in cold water, strain them off, cut away the hard part of the oyster, which must be chopped fine ; then pound eight ounces of cod fish, and put this with the oyster liquor, and two ounces of butter, one teaspoonful of chopped parsley, one of spring onions, and one of mushrooms. Stir all this on the fire, add half a teaspoonful of flour, wet it afterwards with a little vinegar, and let it simmer till nearly all the sauce is reduced. Just before serving add to it the yolks of two eggs diluted with a little milk, and serve.

Iced Savoury Oysters.

Take three or four dozen oysters, and after bearding them and straining their liquor from them, cut them up into small pieces and let them soak in Mayonnaise sauce made with lemon instead of vinegar, for two hours. Have some well-flavoured aspic jelly, and whip it till it is frothy. Put some of this at the bottom of the dish it is to be served in ; then place a layer of the minced oyster, and fill it up with oyster and aspic alternately till the mould is nearly full ; place a stiff band of paper round and fill in with whipped aspic. Put it on ice for two hours ; remove the paper and serve.

Garnish with lemon cut in fancy shapes, and rolled anchovies.

Whole oysters may be used, but that would make the dish very expensive.

Iced Oyster Soufflé.
Soufflé Glacé aux Huîtres.

Prepare the soufflé according to recipe for Oyster Soufflé (p. 43), adding some whipped aspic jelly into the sauce, and after it has steamed and been turned out it should be put into a larger sized mould, which should be filled up with aspic jelly.

Sometimes a few drops of oyster ketchup has been used for flavouring the jelly, but it gives it rather a cloudy appearance. Garnish with chopped aspic, lemon sippets and parsley.

Oysters à l'Indienne.
Huîtres à l'Indienne.

Take one dozen oysters, one dessertspoonful of curry powder, one dessertspoonful of flour, one gill of cream, a little of the oyster liquor, a slice of apple, and half a teaspoonful of lemon-juice. Make the curry sauce, add the oysters, and serve with rice round them.

Oyster Kabobs.

Blanch the oysters in two waters and drain them; put into a stewpan some chopped onions, mushrooms and parsley, with butter and a little flour, and stir in enough yolks of eggs to make the mixture adhere to the oyster. Take some silver skewers, string about six oysters on each silver skewer, the sauce adhering to the oysters and setting around them. Treat with bread-crumbs and eggs, so that the skewers look as if passed through a sausage, and fry a golden brown; dish up on a napkin.

To Keep Oysters.

Put them in a tub and cover them with salt and water. Let them remain for twelve hours, when they should be taken out and allowed to stand for another twelve hours without water. If left without water every alternate twelve hours they will be much better than if constantly kept in water. Never put the same water twice to them.

Oyster Ketchup (Expensive).

Open fifty oysters and preserve all their liquor; add to them half a pound of anchovies, one pint and a half of chablis, and half a lemon sliced, and one quarter of the peel. Let this boil gently for half an hour, then strain it through muslin, add to it cloves and mace, a pinch of each, and half a nutmeg; let it boil a quarter of an hour more, then add to it one ounce of shalots; when cold, bottle it. This is rather an extravagant recipe, but it gives a delicious aroma to white gravies and sauces, &c.

Oyster Ketchup (Brown).

Take half a pint of oysters, save the liquor and scald them in it; let it settle, and strain through a tammy; add to it browning sufficient to colour it. Add two cloves, one blade of mace, a quarter of an ounce of whole pepper, a little salt, cayenne, a clove of garlic, a spoonful of essence of anchovy, and a glass of port wine; boil all together for ten minutes. Strain, and when cold put into well-corked small bottles.

Oyster Ketchup (White).

Take half a pint of fresh oysters, beard them, and boil them gently in their own liquor until all the goodness is drawn out of them. Strain them and put the liquid into a stewpan with half a pint of sherry, six anchovies, a teaspoonful of lemon-juice, and a dozen peppercorns. Let them simmer for half an hour, then strain. Now add two shalots, and boil again for a quarter of an hour, let it get cold, add a teaspoonful of brandy, and when cold, bottle it and resin the corks.

Oyster Kromeskis.

Parboil twelve oysters in their own liquor, beard them, then strain the liquor and cut up the oysters into small dice; melt a piece of butter in a saucepan, stir in a little flour, add the oyster liquor and the oysters, with salt and pepper to taste, and an eggspoonful of chopped parsley. Take the saucepan off the fire, and stir in the yolk of one egg with the juice of half a lemon. When the mixture is cold, divide it into twelve portions; cut some slices of parboiled fat bacon as thin as possible, to the size of an inch and a half by two and a half inches, and wrap each piece tightly in a piece of bacon. When they are all done, dip them in butter and fry them in plenty of hot lard to a pale golden colour. Drain well from fat on a sieve in front of the fire, and garnish with fried parsley.

Huîtres au Lit.

Take two oysters, roll them in a thin broad slice of fat bacon, fasten them with small silver skewers, and roast the tiny roll before the fire in a Dutch oven. Serve on bread sippets. Make as many as there are persons to eat them.

Oysters à la Lucullus.

Blanch two dozen large oysters, and having preserved the liquor, wash and beard them ; put them into a stewpan, adding a dozen stewed mushrooms and a sweetbread blanched and cut into slices ; strain the liquor from the sediment, then add a quarter of a pint of strong veal stock, two spoonfuls of ketchup, one spoonful of lemon pickle, cayenne and salt to taste ; thicken with butter and flour, add a spoonful of browning, and simmer gently for ten minutes. Make a potatoe border, and serve the oysters in the centre, with a garnish of curled anchovies and parsley.

Little Oyster Soufflés à la Sandringham.
Petits Soufflés d'Huîtres à la Sandringham.

Beard a dozen large oysters and cut them up into dice, strain the liquor into a basin ; mix two ounces of Vienna flour with two ounces of butter in a stewpan, a tiny dust of cayenne, a little salt, half a pint of milk, and the yolks of three eggs. Stir and mix these thoroughly together, and stir over the fire till it boils ; add the minced oysters and the liquor. Whip the whites of the three eggs with a pinch of salt till very stiff; then add it to the mixture, mix well together, and fill some little white fireproof china soufflé cups with the mixture. Put a few browned bread-crumbs on the top of each soufflé, and a very small bit of butter, and bake in a moderate oven for a quarter of an hour. Dish up and serve very quickly.

Liver of Herrings with Oysters.

Cut some pieces of bread, three inches long and one wide, half an inch deep, hollow out the centre, fry quite crisp; fill with soft roes of bloaters, with three oysters on each, which must be sautéd in butter for a minute or so. Add just one squeeze of lemon, and a sprinkling of cayenne, and serve very hot.

Oyster Loaves.

Remove a slice from the top of some small loaves, scoop out the crumb from them, and fill them with some oysters just slightly stewed, with butter or cream and a few bread-crumbs ; replace the tops of the loaves, and bake till crisp. The outsides should be glazed with beaten egg.

Oysters and Macaroni.

Lay some macaroni stewed in gravy in a deep dish, place upon it a thick layer of oysters, bearded, and seasoned with cayenne, pepper, and grated lemon-rind ; add a small teacupful of cream, sprinkle bread crumbs thickly on the top, and brown it in a quick oven. Serve hot with piquante sauce.

Oysters à la Maître d'Hôtel.

Huîtres à la Maître d'Hôtel.

Open some large oysters in the deep shells, put over each a little Maître d'Hôtel sauce cold, place them on a gridiron, and serve them the moment the liquor boils. Hand lemon and brown bread and butter with them.

Oysters with Leg of Mutton.

Make half a dozen incisions in the thick part of a leg of mutton, and fill them with a forcemeat made with a dozen fresh oysters boiled in their own liquor for two minutes, then bearded, and minced finely with a shalot, a tablespoonful of scalded and chopped parsley leaves, and the yolks of two hard-boiled eggs. Tie the mutton in a cloth, put it into boiling water, let it boil, then draw it to the side of the fire, and simmer very gently till it is done enough. Serve with oyster sauce.

Oysters au Naturel.

One of the prettiest ways of serving oysters at an oyster supper is to place a little china barrel before each guest, in which are packed a dozen bearded natives; large barrels holding three dozen should be placed on the side table; the lemons cut in quarters and piled high in a dish, garnished with parsley; plates of brown bread and butter around; oyster forks on each plate, with little shells for vinegar, and cayenne glasses.

A coloured glass and a tumbler before each person, and bottles of chablis and stout arranged alternately down the table.

Oyster Omelet (No. 1).

Take twelve good-sized oysters, and mince them very fine ; beat the yolks and whites separately of six eggs, the white until it stands in a firm froth. Now put three tablespoonfuls of butter into a frying-pan, and make it hot. Whilst the butter is heating, stir a cup of milk into the yolks, and season with a little salt, pepper, and a dust of cayenne. Now add in the oysters, stirring well as you add them gradually. When thoroughly mixed pour in a spoonful of the melted butter, then whip in the whites very lightly. If the butter is hot, put the mixture into the pan, and put it over the fire, and when it begins ' to set ' slip a broad-bladed knife round the sides and very cautiously under the omelet, so that the butter may reach every part. As soon as the centre is set, turn it out to a hot dish, with the browned side uppermost.

Oyster Omelet (No. 2).

Break two eggs in a basin, the whites separately ; whip them, adding pepper and salt to taste ; mince parsley enough to fill a teaspoon (fry it for a second in a little butter before mincing). Melt some butter in the omelet pan, and when quite hot, pour in the eggs, and when getting firm put in a tablespoonful of rich oyster sauce, and fold it over and serve.

This omelet is sometimes sent up with a glass of boiling chablis poured round it.

Orlys of Oysters.

Blanch some large oysters, press them slightly between two dishes till cold, then slit them open without quite severing them. Squeeze a little lemon-juice inside, and fold the oysters together again and dip them in some frying batter, and fry in hot fat till they are crisp.

Drain and pile them high on a napkin or paper, and garnish with fried parsley.

D'Uxelles sauce may be served with them.

Oysters in the Pan.
Huîtres au Plat.

Mince a small onion finely, place it in a stewpan with an ounce of butter, a large dessertspoonful of chopped parsley, a little powdered thyme, and pepper and salt to taste. Steam till the onion is tender, then add a quarter of a pint of new milk or cream, and a dozen fresh oysters. Let these get quite hot, then turn them, with the sauce, into one of the china fireproof baking dishes, strew finely-grated bread-crumbs thickly over, and put them into a quick oven till the crumbs are lightly browned. Time altogether, about half an hour.

Oysters en Papillotes.
Huîtres en Papillotes.

Make a paste with cold mashed potatoes, flour and butter. Roll it out and cut it into lozenge-shaped pieces. Put three oysters on each bit of paste, roll it up, and bake a light brown in the oven.

The roll must not be too large ; serve on a napkin very hot.

Oysters and Parmesan Cheese.
Huîtres au Parmesan.

Butter one of the fireproof china dishes, and sprinkle it with browned bread-crumbs. Lay the oysters on this bed of bread-crumbs, strew some finely-chopped parsley and grated Parmesan over them, and then a few more crumbs. Pour in half a glass of chablis and put them in the oven, and pour on a little warm butter whilst in the oven.

Oyster Patties (No. 1).
Petits Pâtés aux Huîtres.

Take two dozen oysters, beard them, and cut them up small, strain the liquor, and put the pieces back into it. Put into a stewpan two ounces of butter, and when it is warmed, dust into it as much flour as it will take up, stirring well all the time, but do not allow it to brown. Then stir in three tablespoonfuls of the liquor from the oysters, and add as much thin cream as will make it the consistency of good butter. Let it simmer till quite smooth, adding to it a dust of cayenne. Add the oysters and give them a warm through, and then leave to cool. Have some little thin paste cases made in dariole moulds ready baked, and fill them with this mixture. Make them very hot and serve. Some prefer the oysters whole, instead of being chopped, with *one drop* of anchovy sauce on each oyster.

Oyster Patties (No. 2. Another Way).

Make some puff paste, roll it out very thin and line some little dariole moulds with it ; fill them with barley or rice to keep their shape, bake them in a brisk oven till cooked. Crush some vermicelli on a board with a rolling-pin, turn out the pastry cases from the moulds, brush them over with white of egg, and roll them in the vermicelli. Take out the rice and fill in an oyster mixture, made of oysters and button mushrooms (two oysters to one small mushroom), all cut into dice. Warm them in a little white sauce, into which a little anchovy sauce and lemon-juice have been added. Make some little paste handles to imitate baskets, and put them across; cover the top with fried parsley and serve very hot. Allemande sauce may be used instead of the white sauce.

Oyster Patties (Old-Fashioned).
Petits Pâtés d'Huîtres à l'Ancien Régime.

Roll out some light puff pastry half an inch thick, stamp it in rounds with a pastry cutter two inches and a half in diameter, press a small cutter an inch and a half in diameter on the middle of each round to the depth of a quarter of an inch. Place the rounds on a buttered tin, and bake them in a quick oven till they are risen, and lightly browned; then take them out, remove the smaller centre-piece, scoop out a little of the inside and fill the empty space with the prepared oysters; put on the lid and serve. Prepare the oysters by bearding them and cutting them into small pieces, with an inch of lemon-rind, a grate of nutmeg, a tiny dust of cayenne and a pinch of pepper, and boil for seven or eight minutes. Strain the liquid, and thicken it with a dessertspoonful of flour and half an ounce of butter. Mix in two tablespoonfuls of

good cream and a dessertspoonful of lemon-juice;
then add the oysters, simmer all together gently
for three minutes, fill the patties and serve.

Oyster Patties à la Française.

Stew some oysters, and beard them, and cut
them into dice.   Have some mushrooms also cut
into dice, which you fry in a little butter dusted
over with flour.   Moisten with some of the liquor
of the oysters, one or two spoonfuls of consommé,
two spoonfuls of cream, and let it reduce.

Add a small bit of butter; season well with
salt and cayenne pepper; throw the oysters into
the sauce and fill the patties, which must be in
dariole moulds.

Oysters and Pheasant.
Faisan farci aux Huîtres.

Stuff a pheasant with three dozen bearded
oysters; put them in as you would stuff a duck, and
hang the bird before the fire exactly in the opposite
position to the usual way.

The oysters give the pheasant a very delicious
flavour.

Oyster Pie.
Pâté d'Huîtres.

Butter the inside of a shallow pie-dish rather
thickly, and line the edges with a good puff paste.
Open and beard two dozen oysters, lay them on
the dish, season with a little salt and cayenne, and
a little grated mace, and sprinkle over them three
tablespoonfuls of finely-grated bread crumbs.   Mix
the strained oyster liquor with a gill of .thick

cream and a teaspoonful of strained lemon-juice. Pour this sauce over the oysters, put the cover over the pie, and bake in a moderate oven.

Oyster Pie à l'Américaine.
(American Recipe.)

Cover a deep dish with puff paste, lay an extra layer around the edge of the plate, and bake nicely. When done fill the pie with oysters (cut off the beards), season with pepper and salt and butter, dust over a little flour, and cover with thin puff paste. Bake quickly; when the top crust is done the oysters should be. Serve as soon as baked, as the crust absorbs the gravy. This pie is quite as good cold as hot.

Oysters Pickled.

Put the oysters which are to be pickled in a saucepan with their own liquor, and let them boil gently for twelve minutes.

Lift them out, put them into small jars and cover them. Let the liquid settle, then pour off the clear part, measure it and put it on to boil with the same quantity of good vinegar, two blades of mace, a teaspoonful of peppercorns, and the thin rind of half a small lemon with each pint of vinegar. Boil this pickle for ten minutes, then take it off, and when cold pour it over the oysters and tie them down carefully, or they will spoil. They will not keep more than a few weeks, therefore they should be put into small jars, so that the contents of one may be finished at once after being exposed to the air. They should be served in a small dish with a little of the pickle strained over them, and a little finely-minced parsley sprinkled on the top.   Brown bread and butter may be eaten with them.

Pillau of Oysters.

Wash six ounces of Patna or Java rice thoroughly and pick out the unhusked grains. Drain it and put it into a saucepan, with a pint of boiling and highly-seasoned gravy.   Keep the pan uncovered ; stir a little at first to prevent the rice from getting into lumps, and let it boil very gently till soft.   Then put it into a sieve, and let the cold water run over it for a few moments ; then place it before the fire to dry.   Keep stirring now and again with a fork to prevent its sticking.   Pile it lightly round a dish, and fill the hollow in the middle with a pint of rich oyster sauce, according to recipe for oyster sauce.

Oyster Powder.

Open three dozen oysters and pound them thoroughly in the mortar with six drachms of salt ; then press them through a hair sieve.   Mix with them as much dried flour as will make them into a smooth paste ; this will be a little more than six ounces.   Roll the mixture out three or four times, and the last time leave it the eighth of an inch thick.   Stamp it into small cakes, dredge these with flour, dry them gradually in a cool oven, and be very careful they do not burn.   To prevent this, turn them every twenty minutes.   When the cakes are quite dry crush them to powder, and put them into bottles, cork and seal them securely, and they will be ready for use when oysters are out of season, when sauces flavoured with oysters are required. For use for sauce, mix three drachms of the powder smoothly with an ounce of butter and six tablespoonfuls of milk ; stir smoothly over a gentle fire till it boils, season with cayenne and lemon-juice.

Oyster Pudding (in Scallop Shells).

Scald the oysters in their own liquor. Take them out, drain, and chop them fine. Take crumb of bread soaked in cream, finely-chopped parsley, chives, anchovy, pepper, and a bit of fresh butter melted to oil. Mix these thoroughly with the chopped oysters, adding at the same time one egg beaten up. Butter the scallop shells and fill them with this mixture. Sprinkle bread-crumbs over the surface, and set them in the oven till delicately browned.

Oyster Puffs à l'Inde.
Talmouse d'Huîtres à l'Inde.

Take two dozen oysters, blanch and beard them, mince them small, and mix them in some clarified butter seasoned with a dessertspoonful of curry paste, a saltspoonful of salt, and the squeeze of a lemon.

Have ready some thin paste, which should be rolled out very thinly and divided into pieces nearly three inches square. Put on each a little of the oyster mixture, and fold them over into three-cornered shapes, wetting the edges and pressing them to make them stick together. Fry these in

D

hot fat till of light brown colour. They should be dished up on a napkin, and sent very hot to table garnished with fried parsley.

Oyster Quenelles.
Quenelles d'Huîtres.

Grate four ounces of the crumb of a stale loaf very finely, add half a teaspoonful of salt, half a teaspoonful of white pepper, half a teaspoonful of pounded mace, a dust of cayenne, two ounces of fresh butter broken into small pieces, the grated rind of half a lemon, and a table-spoonful of chopped parsley. When these ingredients are all thoroughly mixed, stir in a dozen plump oysters which have been bearded and cut into small pieces ; bind it with the yolks of two eggs and the white of one, and a little of the oyster liquid. Pound all these materials until reduced to a smooth paste ; then take a spoon the size required to make the quenelles, and fill it with the forcemeat, and smooth the surface with a knife which has been dipped into hot water. Dip another spoon of the same size into hot water, and with it slip the force-meat out of the first spoon; put it into a buttered dish, and proceed with another quenelle. When as many are made as required, slip the quenelles from the dish into a saucepan of boiling water, and let them poach till firm. Dish them in a circle and mask them with white sauce in which the liquor and some chablis has been strained ; put some of the sauce round, and sprinkle lobster coral and truffle cuttings alternately. Garnish with lemon sippets.

Oyster Ragout.
Ragoût d'Huitres.

Take two dozen oysters ; open them, saving all
the liquor. Make a thick batter with the yolks of
two eggs, a grate of nutmeg, the minced peel of
half a lemon, a spoonful of the juice, a little
flour, and two spoonfuls of milk or cream. Dip
the oysters one by one into this batter, roll them in
bread-crumbs, fry them in butter to a bright brown,
and set them before the fire to keep hot. Have
ready two dozen chestnuts, shelled and skinned, and
fry them in butter. Pour the fat out of the pan,
dredge some flour in, rub a piece of butter over it
with a spoon, put in the oyster liquor, a quarter of a
blade of mace, and half a pint of chablis or vin-de-
grave. Let them boil, thicken the liquor with the
yolks of two eggs, beaten up with four spoonfuls of
cream, and when it is thick pour it over the oysters
and serve.

Oysters à la Reine.
Huîtres à la Reine.

Take a small oval tin about an inch deep,
butter it well all over, and cover with bread-crumbs.
Have ready some good oysters, bearded, and free
from grit ; put a layer of oysters over the bread-
crumbs, shake in a little pepper, repeat the bread-
crumbs with butter over them, and so on till the tin
is full. Pour the oyster liquor (strained) over, and
strew bread-crumbs smoothly at the top ; pour clarified butter over, and brown in the oven for from
fifteen to twenty minutes.

Oyster Rissoles à la Métropole.

Take some large oysters, beard them, and put
into a stewpan four large tablespoonfuls of thick
brown sauce, with half a shalot chopped fine ; season
with a dust of cayenne pepper and half a wine-glass
of chablis or sauterne, and half an ounce of glaze ;
reduce this to half the quantity, skimming it well,
pass it through a sieve, mix in the oysters, and let
it stand to get cool.   Now take some slices of fat
bacon (cooked), stamp them out into little rounds
big enough to hold an oyster, cover each oyster
with some of the brown sauce and place it on the
bacon ; place another round of bacon on the top,
press the edges together, and put it between rounds
of very thin puff paste, pressing the edges well together.   Put them into boiling butter and fry them
a pale yellow colour.   Have some vermicelli rolled
very fine, and dust over them, and then sprinkle
them   alternately   with   lobster   coral   and   dried
parsley ; garnish with lemon.

Oyster Rolls.

Cut some slices of brown bread very thin, butter
them ; place three oysters, over which a little lemon
has been squeezed, a tiny dust of cayenne sprinkled,
and roll them up.   Serve mounted up in a pyramid
on a napkin, garnished with parsley, and celery finely
shred handed with them.

Oyster Roly Poly.

Mix half a pound of flour with a quarter of a
pound of very finely-shred suet, freed from skin

and fibre ; add a pinch of salt, a small egg, and a gill of milk ; roll out three or four times, and then roll it to a long thin form, a quarter of an inch thick and of a width to suit the size of the saucepan in which it is to be boiled ; spread over a layer of minced oysters seasoned with cayenne and lemon-juice, and be careful that it does not reach the edges of the pastry. Begin at one end, and roll it up to fasten the mince inside ; moisten the edges and press them securely together ; dip a cloth in boiling water, flour it well, and tie the pudding tightly in it ; plunge it into a saucepan of boiling water, at the bottom of which a plate has been put, and boil quickly till done enough. Oyster sauce or lemon butter may be served round it.

Oyster Salad.

Open two dozen large oysters, add their liquor to half a pint of dissolved aspic jelly, and the white of an egg beaten up with the shell, mix in a small pan, and place on the stove till it boils ; pass the jelly through a tammy. Take a *casserole* shape, and wet it with cold water, pour in as much jelly as will cover the bottom. Let this set firm, then put in a row of oysters, distant about an inch from each other, and with a spoon pour a little of the jelly over the oysters. Let it get cool. Then have ready some thin slices of beetroot cut lengthways, and with small fancy tin cutters cut out some shapes of beetroot, lay them round in a row the same as the oysters, sauce them over with the jelly, which must be cold but not set. Place alternate layers of oysters, beetroot, and jelly in the mould till it is filled. Put it on ice, and when firm turn it out.

Cut up two lettuces, and mix two tablespoonfuls
of salad-oil with one and a half of vinegar, and a
little pepper and salt ; sprinkle them over the
lettuces and mix them up lightly, and place them
in the centre of the aspic.

Oyster Sandwiches.

Take large stewing oysters, pound them in a
mortar with a little cayenne and lemon-juice, spread
them on thin slices of brown bread and butter, and
cut them into neat little rounds.

Oyster Sauce (Brown).

Allow three oysters for each person, scald them
in their own liquor for two minutes, then beard
them, and if the oysters are large, halve them.   Mix
two ounces of butter very smoothly with an ounce
of flour, add the strained oyster liquor, half a pint of
brown gravy, half a minced shalot, a dust of cayenne,
and a teaspoonful of lemon-juice. Keep stirring till
the sauce is smooth ; then let it boil, after which
put in the oysters, and draw the pan to the side
until they are warmed through, but they must not
be allowed to boil.   A teaspoonful of anchovy is
an improvement, and a tablespoonful of chablis.
Some cooks prefer claret to the chablis.

Oyster Sauce for Entrées.

Having stewed the required number of oysters
in a good lump of butter, and a tablespoonful of
flour in which the liquor of the oysters has been put,
make a white *roux*, into which peel a few ·small

onions and mushrooms, and put them in with the
mixture, as well as a bunch of parsley, and two or
three green onions. Add a few spoonfuls of good
broth or stock, which must be reduced over the
fire. Then add a pint of cream, season well, keep
the sauce pretty thick, strain it through a tammy,
put in the oysters whole, and use it with such
viands as require oyster sauce.

Oyster Sauce à la Jubilé.

Place a pint basin on the kitchen table, and
open the oysters on a little block made for the purpose; pour the liquor into a stewpan, cut off the fat
part of the oyster whilst on the shell into the
basin, then cut off the beard and hard parts, and
place it in the stewpan with the liquor, and proceed
thus till all the oysters are opened. Place the stewpan to simmer for a quarter of an hour, strain off
the liquor and let it stand till it is settled, then strain
it into the stewpan the sauce is to be made in; put in
a quarter to half a pound of butter, a little cayenne,
and thicken with arrowroot, and keep stirring from
left to right till it is done, so that it may be quite
smooth and free from lumps. Just before it is
wanted, pour in the oysters to plump, but not to
boil; then add half a tablespoonful of strained
lemon-juice.

Oyster Sauce à la Savarin.

Take a dozen oysters (or as many more as
required), scald them in their own liquor, and then
strain them. Mix a tablespoonful of flour in the
strained oyster liquor, then mix with this two
ounces of butter, add a dust of cayenne, six drops

of essence of anchovy, and twelve drops squeezed from a lemon. Mix all this smoothly over the fire, and stir till smooth and thick as cream ; put in the oysters, warm well through, and add a gill of good cream. Milk will answer instead of cream for ordinary purposes.

Oyster Sausages.

Take two dozen oysters, beard them and scald them in their own liquor, chop very fine, and mix with five ounces of bread-crumbs, and three ounces of finely-chopped beef suet ; add half a saltspoon of salt, half of pepper, a dust of cayenne, a trifle of grated nutmeg ; pass all this through a wire sieve, or chop very fine and bind the whole with a whole egg ; put it on one side for two hours to cool and to get firm. Flour the hands and make up into cakes or sausages ; flour and fry in butter. If preferred, they can be thrown into boiling water for three or four minutes, drained and left to get cold, then brushed over with egg and bread-crumbs, and lightly broiled or fried.

Savoury Oyster Jelly.

Take a pint of large oysters, and when bearded and the hard parts removed, weigh them, and if they do not weigh a pound, beard some more, till you have the proper weight ; cut them in halves into a stewpan, with their own liquor strained (about half a pint), the strained juice of a lemon, and a teaspoonful of anchovy essence. Let all simmer till all are well amalgamated together, stirring occasionally ; then pass through a sieve. Put one ounce of leaf gelatine into half a gill of water, let it dissolve on the fire, then stir the gelatine strained into the oyster purée. Have some lobster spawn crushed and grated, and sprinkle in some here and there to give it a mottled appearance, and then mould it. Turn out and decorate with crayfish and aspic jelly.

Scalloped Oysters.

Open and beard about eighteen oysters, strain the liquor, and rinse the oysters well in it. Make some thick rich white sauce with milk, butter, and flour, stir the liquor into it, add a little cayenne and a dessertspoonful of lemon-juice, put the oysters in, and let them warm well by the fire, *but not boil*, for four or five minutes. Put the mixture into the shells (scallop shells or silver shells), cover the top with bread crumbs fried a delicate brown and well dried, or put on plain fine bread-crumbs ; pour clarified butter over, and brown with a salamander. Serve very hot and ornament here and there with tiny pieces of parsley. A dessertspoonful of cream put into the white sauce is an improvement.

Scalloped Oysters and Eggs.

Melt two ounces of fresh butter in a saucepan with salt, pepper, a grate of nutmeg, a dessertspoonful of minced parsley, a teaspoonful of minced chives and morells. Well cook this mixture, and scald three dozen oysters in their own liquor (which must be strained) into the mixture, and give one boil up. Then add five or six hard-boiled eggs in slices, simmer over a gentle fire for a few minutes, then pour this into scallop shells,

sprinkle with fine bread-crumbs, lay small pieces of
butter on the top, and brown with the salamander.

Scalloped Oysters à la Française.

Take one dozen and a half oysters, throw
them into boiling water over the fire, and let them
just bubble up, not boil. Roll them in butter (an
ounce of butter for the lot), with a little minced
parsley, pepper and lemon-juice. Make some of
the deep shells quite clean, arrange the oysters
three or four in each, put them on the gridiron, and
the moment the liquor bubbles at the side take
them up and serve them.

Scotch Oysters.

Take one pound of leg of veal, which must be
chopped fine and pounded in a mortar; shred half a
pound of beef suet and add to it; then pound both
together to a paste, add three ounces of fine bread-
crumbs, two whole eggs beaten, a little grate of
nutmeg, and pepper and salt to taste. Shape this
mixture into little flat cakes, fry them in butter or
bake them; now put half a pint of gravy in a small
saucepan, two or three mushrooms, and one dozen
oysters bearded; thicken with a little flour and
butter, bring to the boil, then pour over the cakes
and serve.

Sorrento Oysters.

Stew some macaroni in gravy till tender, seasoning with cayenne and salt to taste; then take
equal parts of oysters and macaroni, and chop them

up together, and mix well in a stewpan with some grated Parmesan cheese, a little butter, and enough cream to moisten all sufficiently ; stir it on the fire till hot, then fill your scallop shells with the mixture and brown them before the fire. Serve immediately.

Oyster Soufflé.

Take two dozen small oysters, mince them, and rub them through a wire sieve. Blanch and beard a dozen large oysters, and cut each one into four pieces. Put two ounces of flour and one ounce of butter into a stewpan, and mix them well together over the fire ; then a quarter of a pint of oyster liquor, and stir all together till it thickens and the flour is well cooked. Put this sauce and the pounded oysters into a mortar and pound them well together, adding the yolks of eggs one at a time, a little salt, cayenne pepper, and a gill of cream ; when these are thoroughly mixed, beat three whites of egg to a stiff froth and stir them into the mixture very lightly ; then put in the oysters. Butter the mould, pour in the mixture, cover it with buttered paper and steam it gently for half an hour ; strew lobster coral over all.

Oyster Soup.

Allow three dozen oysters to a quart of soup. Open them carefully, keep and strain the liquor from them, beard the oysters and put the strained liquor over them. Take a quart of the palest veal stock, and simmer the beards in it for twenty minutes, strain, adding a little more stock if required

Put the oysters over the fire in their own liquor to plump them, but do not let them boil. Put the soup over the fire, add cayenne, and pour the liquor from the oysters to it, and a pint of cream quite hot; put the oysters into the tureen, and pour the soup over them and serve. Thicken with a dessert-spoonful of corn flour, mixed quite smooth with a little milk, and then added by degrees to the soup (letting all simmer together a little). This should be added before the cream. It is better to boil all cream alone before adding it to soups.

Stewed Oysters of the Last Century.

Take two dozen oysters, put them in a stewpan with three ounces of bread-crumbs, add the strained liquor from the oysters, a little mace, also pepper to taste, two ounces of butter, and one tablespoonful of vinegar. Boil all together for a short time, but mind the oysters do not harden. Garnish the dish with fried sippets, and serve very hot.

Oysters Stewed in Wine à la Ronde.

Rub over the bottom and sides of one of the fireproof china dishes with a little butter, lay some oysters in it, strew over them a little pepper and minced parsley, then put to them a small glassful of chablis, cover them with slices of butter cut very thin, strew grated bread over, put a cover on the dish, and set them in the oven with a few hot coals on the cover, and let them cook till they are brown; then take off the fat and serve hot. Half a glass of champagne is preferred by some, but they are more delicate with chablis.

Sweetbreads and Oysters.

Take a calf's sweetbread, soak it in cold water for an hour, and then cut it into pieces about the size of an oyster, and with it two ounces of bacon. Beard a dozen large oysters and mix them with the meat. Sprinkle over all a little pepper and salt, two tablespoonfuls of chopped parsley, a finely-minced shalot, half a teaspoonful of powdered thyme, and four ounces of finely-grated bread-crumbs. Place the sweetbread, oysters and bacon alternately upon small skewers, and serve the oysters &c. on a hot dish. Squeeze the juice of a lemon over them, and pour half a pint of good brown gravy over them.

Oysters en Surprise.

Cut a small slice from each end of four hard-boiled eggs, and cut them into halves the round way. Take out the yolks and pound them in a mortar, and pound in with them a mixture made of one dozen bearded oysters, a little lemon-juice, a dust of cayenne, and half an ounce of butter ; be sure to mix and pound thoroughly. Fill the whites of eggs with this mixture, dish them up, garnished with cut lemon and rolled brown bread and butter.

Oyster Tartlets.

Make some light pastry tartlets, then take some oysters boiled in their own liquor and bearded, one grated spoonful of horse-radish, one gill of stock, some lemon-juice, one tablespoonful of vinegar, one

gill of white sauce, one teaspoonful of capers, half
a gill of the oyster liquor, and a very little salt ; let
all these boil a few minutes. Then add, off the fire,
the yolk of an egg whisked up ; now add the oysters,
then put prawns and pieces of cooked mushroom
in, and then fill up with the oysters and sauce.
Sprinkle over each lobster coral and parsley rubbed
through a sieve.

Make hot in the oven for ten minutes and serve.

Oysters à la Tartare.

Open two dozen native oysters, and scald them
in their own liquor, and then leave them to cool.
Keep one dozen of the lower shells, and select those
which are even at the bottom and will stand steady,
unless silver shells are available. Mix some Mayonnaise sauce made with lemon instead of vinegar,
and add some chopped gherkin and capers. Put
on the bottom of each shell a little mustard and
cress. Remove the beards from the oysters, cut
them in half, and place four half oysters in a pyramid shape on the top of the mustard and cress in
each shell. Just before serving pour some of the
Mayonnaise sauce over each shell of oysters, and
sprinkle a very tiny dust of cayenne on each.
Serve on a flat dish with a napkin garnished with
parsley.

Timbale of Oysters à la Princesse Victoria.

Line a bomb mould very thinly with aspic jelly,
cover some large oysters, some in white sauce
flavoured with their own liquor and lemon-juice, and
some in brown sauce similarly flavoured. Line the

mould with these, alternating the colours, and mask
all over inside with aspic jelly. Prepare a curry mixture similar to ' Oysters curried,' and pour it into the
mould, then put it on ice to get firm ; when ready
turn it out on to a border of iced rice, and garnish
round with sippets of aspic jelly, curled and boned
anchovies, and lemon cut in fanciful shapes.

Oyster Toast.

Pour some well thickened and flavoured oyster
sauce upon a buttered toast, give one squeeze of
lemon and serve very hot.

Oyster Toast à la Gourmet.

Beard and pound a few oysters in a mortar till
they become paste, then add a tablespoonful of
cream, and season with a dust of cayenne. Have
ready some small square pieces of buttered toast,
spread the oyster paste on them, and put them in
an oven for a few moments to warm. Just squeeze
a few drops of lemon through a strainer over them
before serving.

Oyster Trifles.

Take the beards off the oysters and simmer
them for two minutes in two or three tablespoonfuls of water, and strain them ; put the liquor from
the shells and beards to the strained juice of a small
lemon, let it boil, and stir in a tablespoonful of fine
flour, mixed smooth in two tablespoonfuls of milk
or cream ; stir very rapidly for four minutes, as this
sauce will be very thick ; now add an ounce of
butter, and a pinch of cayenne pepper. Chop the

oysters with a silver knife and fork, put them into the sauce, cover the saucepan with its lid, and let it stand on the range for five minutes, taking the greatest care that it does not approach to boiling; the heat of the sauce should be sufficient to cook the oysters—boiling or simmering would simply spoil the dish. Take some little paper cases, which should be less deep than those used for ramekins; take a feather and brush them over with salad-oil, then fill them with the oyster mixture.

Oysters à la d'Uxelles.

Blanch some large oysters, press them slightly between two dishes till they are cold, slit up, then open without quite severing them. Put a quarter of an inch layer of reduced d'Uxelles sauce inside, and fold the oysters together again, press them slightly, then dip them in frying butter, and fry them in hot fat till they are crisp.

Veal and Oysters.

Take two pounds of veal cutlets, cut them into thin pieces, put them in a frying-pan with boiling lard, and let them fry till the veal is half done ; then add a quart of large stewing oysters, their liquor strained and thickened with grated bread-crumbs, and seasoned with a dust of cayenne and a grate of nutmeg. Continue frying till the veal and oysters are thoroughly done, give one squeeze of lemon, and serve garnished with croûtons soaked in lemon-juice and fried.

Oysters à la Villeroi.
Huîtres à la Villeroi.

Blanch some large oysters, warm them in Villeroi sauce, take them out one by one, and coat them thoroughly ; dip them in bread-crumbs and egg, and fry them ; dish them up in a pyramid, and garnish with fried parsley. Villeroi sauce is made with a thickening of butter and flour ; let it be of a good yellow colour. Stir in some fish stock, add a few mushrooms, and a bouquet garni ; simmer for fifteen minutes, pass through a hair sieve, put it in a saucepan again to reduce it, and stir in the yolks of two eggs. Be sure to see the egg does not curdle by cooking it over too fierce a fire.

Vol-au-vent of Oysters.
Vol-au-vent aux Huîtres.

Make the vol-au-vent case in the usual way, and prepare the oyster mixture for the inside thus. Beard two dozen oysters, and put the beards and the liquor into a saucepan with an inch of lemon-rind, a small pinch of salt, half a grain of cayenne, a quarter of an inch of mace, and one grate of a nutmeg. Boil quickly for eight minutes, then strain it. Mix a tablespoonful of flour smoothly with two ounces of butter. Add a gill of cream and the oyster liquor, and simmer gently till the sauce is thick and smooth. Put in the oysters, simmer two or three minutes longer, and serve.

E

Woodcocks and Oysters.
Bécasses à la Poulette aux Huîtres.

Stuff a brace of woodcocks with oysters and roast them, and serve them with a stew of oysters round, prepared by bleaching the oysters in their own liquor, reducing the liquor with a *liaison* of eggs and cream, adding two pats of butter worked with flour, and cooking the oysters in this with pepper and lemon-juice. Serve on toast, and send to table very hot.

SHELLFISH.

—◆◆—

Clam Soup.

WASH as many clams as may be required, and put them into a saucepan with just sufficient boiling water to keep them from burning. Boil them for a few minutes, and when the shells open, and the juice runs out, take the clams from the shells and chop them small. Strain the liquor, and stir into it the chopped clams ; season it with pepper, and thicken with it a little butter, rolled in flour, and let it boil for a quarter of an hour. A little celery or onions may be added, or a little milk, or the yolks of well-beaten eggs.

Stewed Clams (American Dish).

Place the clams in a stewpan with a *little* water, and boil for half an hour, removing the scum carefully ; season the juice with pepper and salt, and serve in the centre of the dish with brown bread and butter sippets around it. Clams can also be fried in batter with egg and bread-crumbs.

Scalloped Collops.

First remove the collops from the shells without tearing them, and then soak in a little weak salt and water to free them from sand and grit. Then parboil them for five minutes in their own liquor, and drain them. Now the liquor from the collops should be put into a small stewpan with a piece of butter, a spoonful of flour, nutmeg to taste, a dust of cayenne pepper, one boned and minced anchovy, and a tablespoonful of cream ; stir this sauce over the fire, and boil for ten minutes, and place the collops back in their respective deep shells. Cover each of them with a good spoonful of the sauce, finish with a layer of fried bread-crumbs. Heat them in the oven and send them to table.

To Cook Cockles.

Wash the cockles in two or three waters, and scrub the shells well, and cleanse them with strong salt and water. Then put them in a clean saucepan, with a tablespoonful of water (if they are to be boiled), and lay a clean towel over them. Shake the saucepan constantly to prevent them burning. As soon as the shells open they are cooked enough. They are best roasted on a tin placed on a stove, and eaten hot with pepper and vinegar, and bread and butter. Cockles may be dressed in all the ways of oysters and mussels, except frying.

Cockle Sauce.

Prepare a gallon of cockles as for boiling. Set them on the fire, and when the shells open, strain the liquid from them, throw the shells away, and strain the liquid through muslin to clean it from sand. Stir in a pint of good melted butter, and add a tablespoonful of vinegar, and half a tea-spoonful of white pepper. Stir the sauce over the fire for two or three minutes, but do not let it boil, and serve it with cod or haddock.

To Dress a Crab.

Take off the large claws, and take out all the flesh of the crab, keeping separate the brownish cream. This brown cream must be mixed with about two good tablespoonfuls of bread-crumbs to a paste ; cut the white meat very small, clear away the fungus part called the ' dead man,' and fill each shell with the white meat, leaving the centre to be filled up with the brown paste. Take the meat out of the claws and shred it finely, and place it on the top of the other white part, and ornament with lobster spawn and sprigs of parsley ; take the feelers off and cut them at both joints, stick the top joint into the joint left on the crab ; chopped aspic jelly and parsley should garnish it. Sometimes the centre of the crab is filled with red imperial Mayonnaise.

Imperial Mayonnaise.

Put into a bowl half a pint of aspic, add to it two spoonfuls of best olive-oil, one of sharp vinegar, and a little salt and cayenne. Break up the jelly quite small with a whisk, stir the ingredients well together, and whisk them till they are converted into a smooth white sauce. It is best mixed over ice. A tablespoonful of cream may be thought an improvement by some, as well as a little flavouring of tarragon and chili vinegar.

A little lobster coral rubbed through a sieve and mixed with it makes it look very pretty.

Buttered Crab.

Pick the meat from the shell of a large crab, mix it with a little salt, pepper, a grate of nutmeg, a spoonful or two of salad-oil, or good cream and vinegar. Be careful to leave out the part near the head, which is not fit to be eaten.

Fill the shell with the mixture, strew finely-grated bread-crumbs over it, and heat it in the oven. Garnish the dish with parsley, and send toasted bread to table with it.

Hot Crab.

Pick the meat out of a crab, clear the shell from the head, then put the meat, with a tiny pinch of nutmeg, a good pinch of pepper, salt, three spoon-fuls of vinegar, some bread-crumbs, and a good bit of butter, into the shell again. Set it before the fire and brown with a salamander.

Crayfish à la Bordelaise.

Pick and wash the crayfish, put them into a stewpan with some French white wine, sliced onions, parsley, salt, pepper, and grated nutmeg; toss the fish over the fire till they are done, then drain and keep them warm.

Cut some carrots and onions in very small dice, fry them in butter till they are coloured, moisten them with chablis, and glaze them ; pour in some Espagnole sauce, and strain in through a tammy the liquor in which the crayfish have been cooked. Reduce the whole, and add some chopped parsley and cayenne pepper. Pile the crayfish high, and pour the sauce over them.

Crayfish (for a Ball Supper Dish).

Take twenty-five crayfish, wash them well, and put them into a three-quart stewpan, with one sliced onion, a handful of parsley, two pinches of salt, and four of pepper, with one gill of chablis or sauterne.

Cover the stewpan, put it on a very brisk fire, boil for ten minutes, tossing the crayfish three times ; when done they should be of a bright red colour. Take out the onion and parsley, drain the crayfish, and dish them on a napkin in the shape of a pyramid ; garnish with fresh parsley.

Lobster Baskets.
Corbeilles au Homard.

Take some hard-boiled eggs and cut them into halves longways. Take out the yolks and pound them in a mortar with the flesh of a hen lobster, two ounces of butter, a grain of cayenne, a teaspoonful of essence of anchovy, and the coral and spawn of the lobster. When well mixed fill the eggs with the mixture. Take some of the claws and put them across to look like a basket handle ; garnish with small salad and aspic. Oysters *can* be dressed thus.

Lobster en Beignets.
Beignets de Homard.

Divide a lobster into as nice pieces as possible, and dip each into a good frying batter, adding to it a little cayenne pepper, and a few drops of essence of anchovies. Fry the *beignet* quickly in good fat, and serve hot.

Lobster Boudinettes.

Pound a lobster, mixing half of the coral with the flesh ; also some prawns or shrimps in equal proportions to the lobster ; an ounce and a half of butter, a saltspoonful of salt, a dust of cayenne ; rub them through a sieve and mould this mixture into some very small *bouchée* cups, heat them in an oven ; roll some powdered lobster over them, and serve with a little rich white sauce coloured with the spawn.

Lobster Creams.

Take the flesh of a lobster, pound it well in the mortar with cream, rub it through a sieve, add an eggspoonful of anchovy sauce, and beat it up well in a pound of Devonshire clotted cream ; put this into the little French white china soufflé moulds ; strew coral over the top and serve.

Lobster Eggs.
Œufs au Homard.

Cut a small slice from each end of some hard-boiled eggs, and cut them into halves the round way. Take out the yolks, and pound them in a

mortar, and blend them well with a mixture made
as follows. Take the flesh of a small lobster, place
it in a mortar and pound it thoroughly with the
hard-boiled yolks of the eggs, and two ounces of
butter, a grain of cayenne, a teaspoonful of essence
of anchovy. When these ingredients are thoroughly
well-mixed and pounded, fill the whites with the
mixture. Place a sprig of watercress in each egg
and garnish with small salad.

Lobster au Gratin.

Split and take all the meat from a good-sized
lobster; cut the meat into dice shapes. Mix all the
coral cream, or soft part, and the inside of the hard,
with half a pint of white sauce, in which a dessertspoonful of anchovy sauce and half a wine-glass of
sherry has been added ; mix in a dust of cayenne.
Put this sauce in a stewpan with the meat, make it
hot, and fill the body shells of three small lobsters
cut in halves ; rasp a few bread-crumbs over each
shell, put a little butter on each to prevent the
crumbs burning, and put them in a Dutch oven
before the fire for five minutes, and serve.

Lobster Quenelles.

Take a freshly-boiled hen lobster, and remove
the meat, pith, coral and spawn. Cut up the tail
into neat scollops and place these in a stewpan
with a little lobster butter ; next place all the re-
mainder of the meat and pith of the lobster in a
mortar, with the flesh of a large whiting, four
ounces of butter, and six ounces of panada ; add
two whole eggs and two yolks. Season with nut-

mcg, cayenne pepper, and a teaspoonful of anchovy. Pound the forcemeat thoroughly, and when well mixed, remove it into a basin; then form the quenelles with a spoon, smooth with a knife dipped in water, and place them in a well-buttered sauté-pan; pour enough light veal or chicken broth over them; let the stock reboil, place a buttered paper over the quenelles, and poach for seven or eight minutes on the side of the stove. Dish them on a potatoe border and serve with Sauce Tartare.

Lobster Rolls.

Cut up a lobster into small pieces, mixing it with all the soft parts of the body.

Make a sauce as follows. Put two ounces of fine flour into a saucepan with a gill of milk or cream, stir over the fire till it begins to thicken; then add two ounces of fresh butter, and work the paste vigorously over the fire until it is well blended. Take off the fire, and add the yolks of two eggs, thoroughly mixing them; add a pinch of cayenne, a few drops of essence of anchovies, and mix the lobster and the sauce together. Roll out puff paste four inches square, put a tablespoonful of the lobster in the centre, fold over so as to form a case, press neatly together and trim the edges. Place on a baking sheet and bake for a quarter of an hour.

Lobster Soufflé à la Kate Terry.

Pound six ounces of lobster and four boned anchovies in a mortar till smooth; add a tablespoonful of anchovy essence, two tablespoonfuls of Devonshire cream, one of Mayonnaise sauce, a tiny dust of cayenne, and some lobster coral, and three-quarters of a pint of aspic jelly ; rub all through a fine hair sieve and whip it till cool. Pour two large spoonfuls of well-whipped cream, one of Mayon-naise sauce, and four of lobster; cut into tiny pieces a pinch of finely-chopped tarragon and chervil. Have ready a little French china soufflé dish, or a silver one about four and a half inches in diameter, and put the mixture into the case. Make a band of paper and surround the case so that it stands about three inches higher than the china. Put it on ice for about an hour, and when ready (it must not be hard) remove the paper, and ornament the top with Mayonnaise sauce and sprinkled lobster coral. Dish it up with cut endive round.

Mussels à la Marinière.

Prepare and cook the mussels as in ' Mussels à la Poulette,' putting a gill more wine over them for boiling them ; when the mussels are done strain the liquor through a strainer into a stewpan. Boil it and add one ounce and a half of butter, and a tablespoonful of chopped parsley ; take it off the fire and stir till the butter is melted. Drain and wipe the mussels, put them on a dish in their shells, pour the sauce over them, and serve. A very small chopped shalot can also be added to the sauce, which is an improvement.

Mussels à la Poulette.

Take one quart of *small* mussels, scrape the shells carefully with a knife, and wash them in several waters. Put a pint of them in a sauté-pan with a sliced onion, a few sprigs of parsley, a pinch of salt, a pinch of pepper, and half a pint of chablis. Cover the sauté-pan, put it on the fire, and toss the mussels occasionally; when the shells are open the mussels are done; take them out and take one shell off. Put the other pint on the fire and cook in the same way. Then strain the liquor into a basin, and put into a stewpan half an ounce of butter, and the same of flour; stir over the fire for three or four minutes, mix the liquor, and add enough water to produce half a pint of sauce; thicken it with the yolk of an egg, and a quarter of an ounce of butter; add a dessertspoonful of chopped parsley.

Dip the mussels in plenty of hot water, drain them well and wipe them. Serve the mussels in their shells, pouring the sauce over them.

Ragout of Mussels.

Cleanse the shells and boil the mussels. When bearded and the black parts are removed, put them into a basin, and the juice which flows from them into another. Dissolve a lump of butter in a stew-pan, mince some parsley, button mushrooms, and two small shalots. Stew them in the butter with a seasoning of pepper and a tiny grate of nutmeg; moisten with the liquor and some gravy. If it be not enough, thicken with flour, and put in the mussels to get hot through, but do not let them boil; a few drops of vinegar improve this dish.

Periwinkle Patties.

Mince some periwinkles previously boiled and taken out of their shells, add a little lemon-juice, some pepper and salt to taste, moisten with a little stock, and a tablespoonful of cream. Make a good puff paste, roll thin, and cut into round pieces; put the paste in patty pans, pour in the mixture and cover with paste. Brush with the yolk of egg and bake.

Coquille of Prawns.

Pick the shells off four dozen prawns, stew them for ten minutes in a sauté-pan in the oven, with three ounces of butter, four truffles, eight button mushrooms sliced, a gill of good clear stock. Fill six scallop shells which have been well buttered, dress each over with fried bread-crumbs, put small dabs of butter on each, and salamander them.

Caviare with Prawns.
Caviar aux Crevettes.

Cut out some little rounds of bread, about two inches in diameter and a quarter of an inch thick, fry them till of a bright gold colour; when cool place on each a piece of caviare and on the top a shelled prawn and shredded chervil. Dish up on a paper.

Croûtes of Prawns à la Tartare.

Cut some halfpenny rolls in half. Take out the crumb whilst hot, and put them in the oven to get hot. Sprinkle with cayenne pepper and salt, and put a little mustard and cress at the bottom of each croûte, and on the top of this put some shelled prawns in the shape of a pyramid. Just before going to table mask them with a spoonful of Sauce Tartare.

Malay Curry of Prawns.

Mince an onion very fine, and put it into a stewpan with a pint or rather more of pickled prawns, and half a stick of cinnamon; pour in a pint of good mutton broth, and season it with salt. Let it stew over a moderate fire for half an hour; then stir in a spoonful and a half of curry powder, and let it stew ten or twelve minutes longer. Strain the gravy into a clean stewpan, add the prawns, and let it simmer again for ten minutes longer. Scrape half a cocoanut into two spoonfuls of water and press it through a sieve. Thicken the milk from the cocoanut with a spoonful of flour, and just before serving the curry stir it into the stewpan, and toss it over the fire for a few minutes. Squeeze in the juice of a lemon and serve it up with boiled rice in a separate dish.

Prawns in Jelly.

Make about a pint and a half of fish jelly, then put some at the bottom of a mould. When cold, lay on it some prawns or crayfish with their backs downwards, and pour more jelly over them; fill the mould in this way, taking care each layer is cool, not cold, before adding more. Place it on ice, and turn it out. Garnish with parsley and prawns.

Prawn Kromeskis.

Mince some prawns, toss them in an ounce of butter, adding a pinch of flour, half a pint of white

stock, salt, pepper to taste. Break up the yolk of
an egg in the juice of a lemon, and mix it with
the prawns. Let the mixture cool, divide it, wrap
each piece in bacon cut thin. Dip each in butter,
and fry for six or seven minutes.

Prawns au naturel à la Mode.

Prawns are generally dressed on a lemon, but
the greatest novelty is to send them up in little
silver shrimp nets ; when they are handed round
at dinners, or at breakfast and lunch, the prawn
nets are simply laid on the table ; hanging to them
are little prawn servers in the shape of boat-hooks.
These are very elegant. The nets can also be
used for watercress.

Prawns en Surprise.

Cut some small rounds of bread and butter, two
inches in diameter, peel some prawns, marinade
them in some Mayonnaise sauce, place three on
each round of bread, with a small piece of watercress
on each ; place over all some whipped aspic jelly.
Strew lobster coral over them, and garnish with
aspic jelly, cut in the shape of lozenges.

Scalloped Scallops.
Coquilles à l'Escalope.

Wash the scallops well in two or three waters,
trim away the beards, preserving the white, black,
and orange-coloured parts. Mince the scallops
finely, and mix with them a very little finely-

chopped parsley, and a little pepper, salt, and a
tiny dust of cayenne. Make a white sauce, cook
it well, add the squeeze of a lemon, then throw the
minced scallops into the sauce for a second, give
one turn on the fire, and pour into the shells ; add six
drops of chili vinegar, strew bread-crumbs over, and
place on the top plenty of little pieces of butter.
Brown with the salamander, and serve very hot.

Croûtes of Shrimps au Diable.

Chop fine sufficient shrimps to fill six croûtes
(*see* Prawns), cook them in a saucepan with a pat
of butter, a dust of cayenne, and a pinch of dry
curry powder. Make hot and fill the croûte with
the mixture, and just before serving add one dessertspoonful of half glaze over each.

Dry Curry of Shrimps.

Dissolve a good slice of butter in a saucepan,
shake it over a brisk fire till it begins to colour,
then put in some picked shrimps and heat them
through. Shake the pan well and turn the shrimps
frequently. When done lift them out, and put into
the saucepan three large onions finely minced, and
a bit of butter, and fry till they begin to soften.
Add a gill of stock, a large sour apple, and juice
of half a lemon, a few pickled gherkins, and two
tomatoes (freed from seeds) ; stew all this till it
becomes thick, put in the shrimps with a dessertspoonful of flour, a teaspoonful of salt and a tablespoonful of curry powder. Simmer softly till the
whole is done, which will be in about three-quarters
of an hour. Serve with rice.

Shrimp Pies.

Pick a quart of shrimps, season with a clove pounded, two anchovies chopped very fine. Put a paste round the edge of mince-pie pans, and a few pieces of butter at the bottom ; then put in the shrimps and more butter, then pour in a glass of white wine, cover them with puff paste, glaze and bake.

Shrimp Timbale à la Irving.
Timbale de Crevettes à la Irving.

Line a mould very thinly with aspic jelly, cut up in strips of about two inches long pieces of lobster flesh, some boned fillets of sardines, anchovies, and beetroot, and arrange these alternately round the mould, and fill up the centre with shrimps. Set the ingredients with more aspic jelly put on ice, and when ready turn out. Dish with whipped aspic round the mould, and very small tomatoes.

Russian Tartlets.
Tartelettes à la Russe.

Make very light pastry tartlets ; then take some oysters scalded in their own liquor (cut off their beards), one grated tablespoonful of horse-radish, one gill of stock, some lemon-juice, one table-spoonful of vinegar, one gill of white sauce, one teaspoonful of capers, half a gill of the oyster liquor, and a very little salt ; let all these boil a few minutes. Then add, off the fire, the yolk of an egg whisked up ; now add the oysters. Then put pieces of lobster, sardines, and anchovies at the bottom of

F

the tartlet-cases, and fill up with oysters and sauce.
Sprinkle over each lobster coral and parsley rubbed
through a sieve, also a few capers. Make hot in
the oven for ten minutes, and serve.

Savoury Brioches.

Take three tablespoonfuls of Mayonnaise sauce,
some celery very finely chopped, a small shalot well
pounded, pieces of lobster, anchovies, and sardines,
also prawns, oysters, and shrimps, a little tarragon
and chervil finely minced. Mix the ingredients
with the Mayonnaise sauce, and fill the brioche-
cases (which are best bought) ; run butter through
the forcer round the edges of the brioche-cases.
Stand them on Montpelier butter (*see* under ' Montpelier Butter' in 'Savouries à la Mode '), strew lobster
coral and boiled yolks of eggs passed through a
sieve on the top of each. Serve with chopped
aspic round.

INDEX.

———•◦•———

Spottiswoode & Co. Printers, New-street Square, London.